Heart of Jesus

Families Novena

Loreto Publications
Fitzwilliam, NH 03447
A.D. 2016

Front cover illustration: Chambers, Sacred Heart
End sheet images taken from Depiction of the Heart
of Jesus drawn by Saint Margaret Mary Alacoque
herself.

Original German title:
*Novene zum göttlichen Herzen Jesu mit der heiligen
Margareta Maria Alacoque*
© 2015 by Sarto Verlagsbuchhandlung GmbH,
Stuttgart, Germany

© 2016 English Edition by
Loreto Publications
P. O. Box 603
Fitzwilliam, NH 03447
603-239-6671
www.loretopubs.org

ISBN: 978-162292-102-7

English Translation by Michael Miller

Unless otherwise indicated, citations from the works
of Saint Margaret Mary Alacoque are taken from The
Autobiography of Saint Margaret Mary, translated
by the Sisters of the Visitation in Roselands (Kent,
England, 1930) and from Fr. John Croiset, S.J., The
Devotion to the Sacred Heart of Jesus, translated
by Fr. Patrick O'Connell, B.D. (St. Paul, MN: The
Radio Replies Press Society, 1959).

Heart of Jesus Families Novena

According to the revelations of the Sacred Heart
and with prayers composed by
Saint Margaret Mary Alacoque

For the spread
of the kingdom of the love
of the Sacred Heart of Jesus,
so as to renew all things in Christ

This novena also serves
as the Perpetual Novena
of the Sacred Heart of Jesus Families

Apparition of the Sacred Heart of Jesus
to Saint Margaret Mary Alacoque,
Mosaic by Carlo Muccioli,
Saint Peter's Basilica, Vatican City

Table of Contents

Introduction

The Importance of Devotion to the Sacred Heart of Jesus in our Time

Honoring the Most Sacred Heart of Jesus is more than a devotional practice. In the Heart of Christ, we honor the most profound mystery of His divine-human love: the love of God which, in the God-man Jesus Christ, was sacrificed for us even unto death to redeem us from our sins and thereby to reconcile and unite us again with God.

Therefore, this love of God also demands a response: our love in return, and the surrender of our heart. Consequently, this devotion is something profoundly interior; it consists of the deepening of our relationship to Christ, and touches on the most essential elements of our religion: union with God, and life with Him and in Him.

Why is devotion to the Heart of Jesus necessary, especially today, to promote our eternal salvation? There are three reasons to consider:

1. To Rekindle our Love for God

"God is love," Saint John teaches; and in the Christmas liturgy we hear the consoling words: "The goodness and kindness of God our Saviour has appeared.... According to His mercy, He saved us." [See Titus 3:4-5.] Today, to a great extent, the awareness of God's love has been lost, and His goodness has been forgotten. Because of selfishness and materialism, even many Christians have no true love for God, and the very concept of love is frequently distorted into a merely emotional matter. For this reason, Christ foretold the devotion to His Heart to Saint Gertrude (+1302) as a remedy for our time, when faith would become shallow and love would grow cold. She writes in her work, Herald of Divine Love: "My mission was to write of the Eternal Word.... The language of the blissful pulsations of the Sacred Heart is reserved for latter times, that the time-worn world, grown cold in the love of God, may be warmed up by hearing of such mysteries."

The revelations of the Heart of Jesus to Saint Margaret Mary Alacoque confirm this promise: "Behold this Heart which has so loved human beings that It has spared nothing, even to exhausting and consuming Itself, in order to give them proof of Its love." These words testify to the infinite love of Jesus. In a visible way, God shows us in Jesus that there is a place in His Heart for us, and that is the strongest incentive for us really to love God as well.

2. To Restore the Reign of Christ the King

Today, as a result of wiles and machinations, unbelief has made such headway that Christ's legitimate kingship over society is denied and even opposed. Shouting the battle cry, "We do not want Him as our King!", Christ's enemies have literally dethroned Him. If Christ does not rule, though, Satan will immediately claim His place. We are currently experiencing the devastating consequences of this de-Christianization. Through devotion to the Sacred Heart of Jesus, especially through the consecration associated with it, we once again pledge to our King the love of our hearts, acknowledge His kingship over us and thus set it up again in miniature in society. Christ promised Saint Margaret Mary: "Fear not, I will reign in spite of My enemies and all who oppose it."

3. To Make Reparation for Blasphemies Against Christ

The public insults and crimes against Holy God provoke the divine justice. The outrages committed against God through men's misdeeds must be atoned for, and the disrupted order must be restored through penance. The reparation that is an essential part of devotion to the Sacred Heart of Jesus, in union with Christ's atoning sacrifice, works to turn aside or at least to mitigate the punishments that they have deserved. In the message of Our Lady of Fatima, which has Church approval, the call to make reparation was even more insistent, inasmuch as reparation for the offenses against the Immaculate Heart of Mary was demanded as well. The Angel of Peace taught the three shepherd children the well-known prayer of atonement: "My God, I believe in You, I adore you..." (see p. 56).

In a later apparition, he recited for them the prayer to the Most Holy Trinity and administered to them a communion of reparation with the words: "Receive the Body and drink the Blood of Christ, who is terribly offended by ungrateful men. Make reparation for their sins and console your God." Because these sins have reached critical mass today, the duty to make reparation is all the more urgent.

Margaret Mary Alacoque and the Heart of Jesus

The saintly nun, Margaret Mary Alacoque (1647-1690), received from Christ abundant revelations about the mystery of His divine Heart. Her mission was confirmed by Him with the significant words: "I make you heiress to the treasures of My Heart. You may dispose of them at will in favor of those who are properly disposed."

She recorded her visions and their supernatural instructions in an autobiography and in many letters. The Magisterium of the Church examined these revelations, approved them, and emphasizes that this is not a special devotion. Devotion to the Heart of Jesus and the liturgical feast of the Sacred Heart are not the memorial of a particular mystery of salvation, but rather the summary of all other feasts, which celebrate individual mysteries from the life of Christ, for every mystery of redemption is a mystery of love. The purpose of honoring the Heart of Jesus is to celebrate solemnly this mystery of His love. Consequently, we can say that this devotion is the summary of the whole Catholic faith.

The essential elements of the devotion to the Sacred Heart of Jesus are explained for us in the revelations to Saint Margaret Mary:

- ♥ its origin: the infinite, overflowing love of the Son of God, which makes one last effort to save sinners;
- ♥ its object: the physical Heart of Christ as the vessel of His divine love, which moves this Heart;
- ♥ its goal: to render love, atonement and reparation to the Heart of Jesus, which has been misunderstood and wounded by the sins of mankind;
- ♥ its effects and fruits: a superabundant outpouring of divine love and mercy, which converts sinners, inflames lukewarm souls, leads the zealous to sanctity, and thus renews the Church for the salvation of the whole world.

For a Better Understanding of the Prayers of Saint Margaret Mary Alacoque

From her childhood, Saint Margaret Mary was admitted to the school of the divine Heart and was gradually raised by the Savior to the heights of the spiritual life. She experienced many purifications, and finally mystical marriage with the Savior. Our Lord honored her with the name of "much beloved disciple of His Heart". She was tested by sufferings, and through humility and love for the Cross even unto total self-surrender to the divine Heart of Jesus, she was led to the highest degree of perfection. As a result of her deep knowledge of God and her ardent love for the divine Savior, she arrived at a profound concept of human unworthiness and sinfulness. For this reason, her prayers may sometimes seem to our imperfect sensibilities exaggerated and difficult to understand.

Here it is important to ponder what the author of *The Imitation of Christ* teaches: "Son, you must not be frightened off or discouraged when you hear what the way of perfection is; but rather be incited thereby to undertake great things, or at least to sigh after them with an earnest desire." *(The Imitation of Christ,* Book 3, Chapter 32).

The texts cited in this little book were taken mainly from the French edition of the complete works of Saint Margaret Mary: *Vie et oeuvres de sainte Marguerite-Marie Alacoque,* 3 vols. (Paris, 1920), published by Archbishop Gauthey of Besançon. The prayers are found in Volume 2 of this edition on pages 777-820; the English translation thereof is taken from the appendix to the book by Fr. Croiset, S.J., *The Devotion to the Sacred Heart of Jesus* (St. Paul, MN: The Radio Replies Press Society, 1959).

The Spiritual Fruits of Devotion to the Sacred Heart of Jesus

The following novena is composed of selected passages from the revelations of the Heart of Jesus and the prayers of Saint Margaret Mary Alacoque. On each day of the novena, a theme from devotion to the Sacred Heart of Jesus is presented for meditation and developed with appropriate prayers. In this way, we become acquainted with the wealth of graces contained in this good news, that is, the infinite love and kindness of Jesus Christ and the immeasurable treasures of His divine Heart, and learn to make use of them for our sanctification. Our Lord's words to the Saint are instructive, consoling, and at the same time stimulating; they invite us to trust and to surrender to the merciful love of God. Because these teachings contain such great wealth, we should constantly seek a deeper understanding of them through contemplative prayer. In that way, our souls can be formed in the Christian spirit; this fosters the virtues of faith, humility, trust in God, adoration, love, willingness to sacrifice, and surrender to God.

As the finest fruit, we hope for what the Epistle from the Liturgy of the Feast of the Sacred Heart of Jesus expresses in the words of Saint Paul: "May the Father of our Lord Jesus Christ . . . grant you, according to the riches of his glory, to be strengthened by his Spirit with might unto the inward man: that Christ may dwell by faith in your hearts: that, being rooted and founded in charity, you may be able to comprehend, with all the saints, what is the breadth and length and height and depth, to know also the charity of Christ, which surpasseth all knowledge: that you may be filled unto all the fulness of God" (Eph 3:16-19).

Stages Leading to the Church's Approval of the Sacred Heart Devotion

On December 27, 1673, in Paray-le-Monial, the Lord appeared to Sister Margaret Mary Alacoque (now canonized), of the Visitation Order founded by Saint Francis de Sales, and revealed to her His message about honoring His Most Sacred Heart. Further revelations followed in the years 1674 and 1675.

In the year 1856 Pope Pius IX prescribed the liturgical Feast of the Sacred Heart of Jesus for the entire Catholic Church.

On May 25, 1899, Pope Leo XIII announced the consecration of the world to the Most Sacred Heart of

Jesus, which was accomplished on Sunday, June 11, 1899, in all the Catholic churches of the world.

On January 10, 1915, the German bishops unanimously carried out the consecration of Germany to the Most Sacred Heart of Jesus.

The Feast of the Sacred Heart of Jesus is celebrated as a first-class feast on the Friday of the week after Corpus Christi, which is the third Friday after Pentecost.

Note on Fasting

Someone who considers himself capable of doing so can supplement the novena prayer of reparation with several days of fasting, for example on the Fridays that fall in the time of the novena. Fasting is refraining from food and drink out of love for God. The Church's definition of fasting is to take only one full meal on a given day, whereby two small snacks are permitted. In making plans to fast, one should seek the advice of his confessor, for prudence is needed in this matter. Fasting cannot replace the penances that God demands of us in the first place: the faithful, daily fulfillment of the duties of our state in life in our family and in our work. It will be pleasing to God as an additional sacrifice, however, if we fast in such a way as to be able to fulfill the duties of our state in life as well. When a person cannot fast, for example because of the rules of community life, one can nevertheless impose sacrifices on oneself by choosing foods that are less to one's taste.

Why Fast?

For the glory of God and for the salvation of souls/the conversion of sinners.

"... this kind is not cast out but by prayer and fasting" (Matthew 17:21).

To uplift the mind and to prepare for special days (e.g. major feast days).

The Sacred Heart of Jesus is already pleased by little acts of self-denial.

"Publish this devotion everywhere, propagate it, recommend it to people of the world as a sure and easy means to obtain from Me a true love of God; to ecclesiastics and religious, as an efficacious means to arrive at the perfection of their state; to those who work for the salvation of their neighbor, as an assured means to touch the most hardened hearts; and finally to all the faithful, as a most solid devotion, and one most proper to obtain victory over the strongest passions, to establish union and peace in the most divided families; to get rid of the most long-standing imperfections; to obtain a most ardent and tender love for Me; in short, to arrive in little time and in a very easy manner, at the most sublime perfection."

Words of the Lord to St. Margaret Mary, recorded by her confessor, Fr. Jean Croiset, S.J., in his book, *The Devotion to the Sacred Heart of Jesus* (Rockford, IL: Tan Books and Publishers, Inc., 1988), 80.

Depiction of the Sacred Heart of Jesus in the
Church of the Gesù, Rome.

Novena to the Sacred Heart of Jesus

We begin each day with the following offering and prayer:

O Most Sacred Heart of Jesus, King of all hearts, I consecrate my heart to You today and place it entirely at Your service. I offer to You my soul with all its faculties and my body with all its senses. I wish to spend my whole life loving You, serving You and following You. I resolve to be a zealous worshipper of the sacrament of Your love.

Immaculate Heart of Mary, after the Heart of Jesus the most perfect and lovable heart, you too shall be the perpetual object of my reverence and love. Teach me to honor the Heart of your Divine Son, as you yourself honored it, and allow me to offer to Him your adoration and love.

O Jesus, to Your divine Heart I commend *(that soul..., a concern..., this trouble)*. I trust in You, I abandon myself entirely to Your Divine Providence and I am sure that You will hear and answer my prayer.

Most Sacred Heart of Jesus, may Your kingdom come to us. Your will be done, on earth as it is in heaven. Amen.

Then read the meditation for the day and recite the accompanying prayers. If several prayers are given, it is permissible for a sufficient reason to choose only one.

We should also be mindful of the fact that it is better and in God's sight certainly more pleasing to do a little less but with more devotion, zeal and love for God and—if grace prompts us—to pray in the ardor of the heart, than to rattle off as many prayers as possible but to recite them with a lack of devotion. Here too it is true: less is sometimes more. In order to enter into the spirit of devotion to the Sacred Heart of Jesus, contemplative prayer practiced in the stillness of the heart is of great importance.

"This is the will of God, your sanctification" (1 Thess. 4:3; Eph. 1:4). Let us make an effort and bring ourselves to pray often together with others, too: "If two of you shall consent upon earth concerning any thing whatsoever they shall ask, it shall be done to them by my Father who is in heaven" (Mt. 18:19). It brings additional graces, fosters mutual support, and gladdens the Heart of Jesus in a special way, since It loves the unity of hearts so much.

Day One

The Redeemer Desires to Save the World Through the Mercy of His Most Sacred Heart

Meditation

"One day... [when] I was praying before the Blessed Sacrament..., He made me repose for a long time upon His Sacred Breast, where He disclosed to me the marvels of His love and the inexplicable secrets of His Sacred Heart, which so far He had concealed from me.... My divine Heart, He said, is so inflamed with love for men, and for thee in particular that, being unable any longer to contain within Itself the flames of Its burning Charity, It must needs spread them abroad by thy means, and manifest Itself to them (mankind) in order to enrich them with the precious treasures which I discover to thee, and which contain graces of sanctification and salvation necessary to withdraw them from the abyss of perdition...."

Revelation of the Sacred Heart to St. Margaret Mary on December 27, 1673

Consideration

The Savior points to His Heart as the quintessence of His infinite love for us sinners. His loving Heart is also the source of the richest graces. It is capable of healing all our failings and weaknesses and of helping us in all our needs. Therefore let us have recourse to It.

Salutations to the Sacred Heart of Jesus

Hail, Heart of Jesus! Save me.

Hail, Heart of my Creator! Perfect me.

Hail, Heart of my Saviour! Deliver me.

Hail, Heart of my Judge! Pardon me.

Hail, Heart of my Father! Govern me.

Hail, Heart of my Spouse! Love me.

Hail, Heart of my Master! Teach me.

Hail, Heart of my King! Crown me.

Hail, Heart of my Benefactor! Enrich me.

Hail, Heart of my Pastor! Guard me.

Hail, Heart of my Friend! Caress me.

Hail, Heart of my Infant Jesus! Draw me to Thee.

Hail, Heart of Jesus, dying on the Cross! Ransom me.

Hail, Heart of Jesus, in all Thy states! Give Thyself to me.

Hail, Heart of my Brother! Dwell with me.

Hail, Heart of incomparable goodness! Pardon me.

Hail, Magnificent Heart! Shine forth in me.

Hail, Most Amiable Heart! Embrace me.

Hail, Charitable Heart! Operate in me.

Hail, Merciful Heart! Answer for me.

Hail, Most Humble Heart! Repose in me.

Hail, Most Patient Heart! Bear with me.

Hail, Most Faithful Heart! Atone for me.

Hail, Most Admirable and Most Worthy Heart! Bless me.

Hail, Peaceful Heart! Calm me.

Hail, Most Desirable and Excellent Heart! Enrapture me.

Hail, Illustrious and Perfect Heart! Ennoble me.

Hail, Sacred Heart, Precious Balm! Preserve me.

Hail, Most Holy and Profitable Heart! Make me better.

Hail, Blessed Heart, Medicine and Remedy of our evils! Cure me.

Hail, Heart of Jesus, Solace of the afflicted! Console me.

Hail, Most loving Heart, burning Furnace! Consume me.

Hail, Heart of Jesus, Model of perfection! Enlighten me.

Hail, Heart of Jesus, Origin of all happiness! Fortify me.

Hail, Heart of eternal blessings! Call me to Thee.

St. Margaret Mary Alacoque, Prayer No. 2, translated from collected works Vie et Oeuvres, volume 2, edited by François Léon Gauthey (Paris: Ancienne Librairie Poussielgue, 1920).

Most Sacred Heart of Jesus, I place my trust in You!

Thought for the day

"Proclaim, and have it proclaimed to the whole world, that I set no limit on My gifts of grace for those who seek them in My Heart."

Jesus to Saint Margaret Mary

Most Sacred Heart of Jesus, make my heart like
Yours.

Day Two

Jesus Invites us to Unite our Hearts with His

Meditation

"After this He asked me for my heart, which I begged Him to take. He did so and placed it in His own adorable Heart where He showed it to me as a little atom which was being consumed in this great furnace, and, withdrawing it thence as a burning flame in the form of a heart, He restored it to the place whence He had taken it, saying to me: See, My well-beloved, I give thee a precious token of My love, having enclosed within thy side a little spark of its glowing flames, that it may serve thee for a heart and consume thee to the last moment of thy life.... I now give thee the name of the beloved disciple of My Sacred Heart."

From the Revelation on December 27, 1673

Consideration

Our Lord Jesus Christ calls to us: "I am come to cast fire (the love of God) on the earth. And what will

I, but that it be kindled?" May this fire of divine love seize, sanctify and inflame our hearts.

Prayer to the Sacred Heart of Jesus in Every Need

From the profound abyss of my nothingness, I prostrate myself before Thee, O most Sacred, divine, and adorable Heart of Jesus, to render Thee all the homage of love, praise, and adoration of which I am capable, and to present to Thee my necessities, both spiritual and temporal, discovering to Thee as to my most perfect friend, all my miseries, my poverty, my nakedness, my infirmity, my pusillanimity, in short, all the wounds and ulcers of my soul, begging Thee to have compassion on me and graciously to help me according to the greatness of Thy mercies, which Thou makest Thy glory to show us in our extreme necessities. O Heart all good, my only hope is in Thee. Save me, I Implore Thee, by all that is most capable of moving Thee to grant this favor to me and to all those who are in the same peril of their salvation. Oh! Do not allow me to perish in the deluge of my iniquities; provided that I love Thee eternally. For the rest, do what Thou willest with me and in me.

I have placed all my confidence in Thee, do not reject me. I call Thee, I invoke Thee, as the sovereign remedy for all my evils, the greatest of which is sin. Destroy it in me and grant me pardon for all the sins that I have committed, of which I repent with my whole heart, and ask Thy forgiveness for them.

Make then Thy sovereign power, O loving Heart, felt by me and by all hearts capable of loving Thee, especially by my parents and friends, and by all those persons who have recommended themselves to my

8

prayers or who are praying for me, and by any for whom I have a special obligation. Assist them, I beseech Thee, according to their necessities.

O Heart full of charity, soften hardened hearts and relieve the souls in Purgatory; be the assured refuge of those in their last agony and the consolation of all those who are afflicted or in need. In short, O Heart of love, be to me all in all things; but especially at the hour of my death, be the safe retreat for my poor bewildered soul. At that moment, receive it into the bosom of Thy mercy. Amen.

St. Margaret Mary Alacoque, Prayer no. 26.

Most Sacred Heart of Jesus, I place my trust in Thee!

Thought for the day

"I doubt whether there is any exercise of piety in the spiritual life as well adapted to raise a soul to the highest perfection in a short time and to make it taste the true sweetness one finds in the service of Jesus Christ."

St. Margaret Mary Alacoque

Day Three

Jesus Wants us to Honor His Love Under the Image of His Heart

Meditation

"The divine Heart of Jesus was shown to me as on a throne of flames, more dazzling than the sun and transparent as crystal, with that adorable wound, and surrounded with a crown of thorns signifying the pricks caused to it by our sins; and above there was a cross, which meant that from the first moment of His Incarnation the cross was planted in it.... And He showed me that it was His great desire of being loved by men and of withdrawing them from the path of ruin into which Satan hurls such crowds of them, that made Him form the design of manifesting His Heart to men.... He should be honored under the figure of this heart of flesh, and Its image should be exposed. He wished me to wear this image on my own heart, that He might impress on it His love and fill it with all the gifts with which His Heart is replete, and destroy in it all inordinate affections. He promised me that

11

wherever this image should be exposed with a view to showing It special honor, He would pour forth His blessings and graces."

Quotation from the description of the revelation in 1674 of the promises for the nine First Fridays.

Consideration

The image just described of the Heart of Jesus makes the Redeemer's love and suffering visible. When we contemplate it, we are once again reminded of them and incited to grateful veneration and loving confidence.

Act of Adoration to the Sacred Heart

With all the power of my heart, I now adore Thy sovereignty, O most Sacred, divine, and adorable Heart of Jesus, whom I wish to fear and respect with continuous attention, never more to offend Thee, because Thou art infinitely good. O most Sacred Heart, I love Thee and wish to love Thee above all things with all my strength and power. I detest every mortal sin and all voluntary venial sins; I hope that as we belong to Thee, who hast given birth to us on the Cross with so much pain, Thou wilt have pity on our weakness and misery and not allow us to perish.

I offer myself entirely to Thee, O Heart of love, with the intention that my whole being, my life and my sufferings, may be employed in loving, honoring, and glorifying Thee, in time and in eternity. I love Thee, O most amiable Heart, as my sovereign good, my entire happiness and all my joy, as the sole object worthy of the love of all hearts. May my heart be reduced to cinders by the ardor and vehemence of this love, by which I renew with my whole soul all the offerings which I have made to Thee of myself. Keep me from displeasing Thee and grant me to do what is most pleasing to Thee. O Heart, source of pure love, would that I might be all heart to Thee and all soul to adore Thee! Grant that by Thy holy grace, I may be able to love only Thee, to love in Thee and by Thee and for Thee. May my memory think only of Thee, may I have no other understanding but to know Thee, no other will or affection but to love Thee, no tongue but to praise Thee, no eye but to see Thee, no hands but to serve Thee, no feet but to seek Thee, in order that I may be able one day to love Thee without fear of losing Thee for all eternity. Amen.

St. Margaret Mary Alacoque, Prayer no. 28.

Prayer to the Most Sacred Heart of Jesus

O loving Heart of Our Lord Jesus Christ, O Heart which woundest hearts harder than stone, which warmest souls colder than ice and softenest feelings more impenetrable than diamond, wound my heart by Thy sacred wounds, O my amiable Saviour, and inebriate my soul with Thy Blood, so that whatever side I may turn, I may see nothing but my divine Crucified Saviour, and that everything I look upon may appear stained with Thy Blood. O my good Jesus, grant that my soul may not repose until it has found Thee, who art its center, its love and its happiness.

My amiable Jesus, by the Sacred Wound of Thy Heart, pardon me all the sins I have committed through malice or through impure intentions. Put my wicked heart in Thy divine Heart, in order that being continually under Thy protection and direction, I may persevere constantly in doing good and avoiding evil until I breathe my last sigh.

St. Margaret Mary Alacoque, Prayer no. 8

Most Sacred Heart of Jesus, I place my trust in Thee!

Thought for the day

"Jesus promised me that He would abundantly pour out all the treasures of graces with which His Heart is filled into the hearts of those who honor the image of His Most Sacred Heart."

Promises to St. Margaret Mary

Day Four

Jesus Longs for our Love in Return

Meditation

"One of my greatest sufferings was caused by this divine Heart addressing to me these words: 'I thirst with such a terrible thirst to be loved by men in the Blessed Sacrament that this thirst consumes Me. Yet I find no one trying to quench it according to My desire by some return of My love.'"

Letter no. 133a of St. Margaret Mary to Father Croiset, November 3, 1689

Consideration

Jesus, whose Heart beats for us, desires that we human beings worship His divine love under the image of His Heart and return this love, which is still living among us in the Most Blessed Sacrament of the altar. How could this plaintive, earnest request of our Lord fail to touch our hearts and move us to respond to it as well as we can?

Prayer of Love to the Sacred Heart

O Heart of Jesus all inflamed with love and living by love, O Sanctuary of the Divinity, Temple of His Sovereign Majesty, Altar of divine Charity, O Heart burning with love for God and for me, I adore Thee, I love Thee, I melt with love and reverence before Thee! I unite myself with Thy holy dispositions, I desire most earnestly to burn with Thy fire and to live by Thy life. What joy is mine to see Thee well pleased and content. Thou hast lavished Thy graces upon me and made me share in Thy sorrows and in Thy glory. Oh! how I would willingly die or suffer anything rather than displease Thee!

O my heart, you must act only by the impulses from the Sacred Heart of Jesus; before It, you must expire in silence to all that is human or natural.

O divine Heart, I unite myself with Thee, and lose myself in Thee. I do not wish to live any longer but in Thee, by Thee, and for Thee. Thus all my employment shall be to remain in silence and respect, annihilated before Thee like a burning lamp which is consumed before the Blessed Sacrament; to live, to suffer, and to die. Amen.

St. Margaret Mary Alacoque, Prayer no. 23

Saint Margaret Mary's Prayer of Offering

Eternal Father, I offer unto Thee the infinite satisfaction which Jesus rendered to Thy justice on behalf of sinners upon the tree of the Cross; and I pray that Thou wouldst make the merits of His Precious Blood available to all guilty souls to whom sin has brought death; may they rise again to the life of grace, and glorify Thee for ever.

Eternal Father, I offer Thee the fervent devotion of the Sacred Heart of Jesus in satisfaction for the lukewarmness and cowardice of Thy chosen people, imploring Thee by the burning love which made Him suffer death, that it may please Thee to rekindle their hearts now so lukewarm in Thy service, and to set them on fire with Thy love, that they may love Thee for ever.

Eternal Father, I offer Thee the submission of Jesus to Thy will, and I ask of Thee, through His merits, the fullness of all grace and the accomplishment of all Thy holy will. Blessed be God! Amen.

St. Margaret Mary Alacoque

Most Sacred Heart of Jesus, I place my trust in Thee!

Thought for the day

"He showed me many names written on His Heart, of those who wished to make Him known, loved and honored. Therefore He will never allow them to be erased from It."

Promises to St. Margaret Mary

Day Five

The Savior Calls us to Make Atonement

"Jesus Christ, my sweet Master . . . showed me His loving and lovable Heart as the living source of those flames of His divine love. Then he revealed to me all the unspeakable marvels of His pure love, and the excess of love He had conceived for men from whom He had received nothing but ingratitude and contempt. 'This is more grievous to Me,' He said, 'than all that I endured in my Passion. If they would only give Me some return of love, I should not reckon all that I have done for them, and I would do yet more if possible. But they have only coldness and contempt for all My endeavors to do them good. You, at least, can give Me the happiness of making up for their ingratitude, as much as you can.'"

Testimony of St. Margaret Mary

Consideration

Obviously this is not about the sufferings that our Savior endured in His Passion, but rather about the humiliation and insults that are inflicted on Him today. Today especially, when His Most Sacred Heart is so grievously offended by the many souls that have fallen away from the faith, It deserves in a special way our adoration, love, and reparation.

Prayer of Adoration and Love to the Sacred Heart

I adore Thee, I love Thee, I praise Thee, I cry to Thee for mercy, I return Thee thanks, I invoke Thee, and confide myself entirely to Thee, O most holy and adorable Heart of my Lord and Saviour Jesus Christ, who, for the salvation of us all, didst submit Thyself to the rigors of divine justice, and didst voluntarily accept a birth accompanied with poverty, sorrow, and contempt, a life of labor and contradictions, but of kindness for all, and a death full of opprobrium, confusion, and sorrow, and who, in short, for the love of those who wish to be saved through Thy divine charity, dost remain in the Blessed Sacrament of the altar to the end of time. Accomplish, O most adorable Heart, Thy wishes in my poor and miserable heart, which I dedicate and consecrate to Thee forever. Grant that it may live in the sentiments of love and gratitude which it owes Thee, that it may at all times breathe only Thy honor and glory, in order that it may expire in the waters of perfect contrition. Amen.

St. Margaret Mary Alacoque, Prayer no. 27

Prayer of Adoration to the Blessed Sacrament

Jesus Christ, my Lord and my God, whom I believe to be really present in the Blessed Sacrament of the altar, receive this act of most profound adoration to supply for the desire I have to adore Thee unceasingly, and in thanksgiving for the sentiments of love which Thy Sacred Heart has for me in this sacrament. I cannot better acknowledge them than by offering Thee all the acts of adoration, resignation, patience, and love which this divine Heart has made during Its mortal life, and which It makes still and will make eternally in Heaven, in order that through It, I may love Thee, praise Thee, and adore Thee worthily as much as it is possible for me. I unite myself to this divine offering which Thou dost make to Thy divine Father, and I consecrate to Thee my whole being, praying Thee to destroy in me all sin and not to permit that I should be separated from Thee eternally. Amen.

St. Margaret Mary Alacoque, Prayer no. 24

Most Sacred Heart of Jesus, I place my trust in Thee!

Thought for the day

"My heart expected reproach and misery; I looked for sympathy, but there was none; and for comforters, and I found none."

Offertory for the Feast of the Sacred Heart of Jesus;
Psalm 68:21

St. Margaret Mary Alacoque / (authentic image) /
July 22, 1647 – October 17, 1690

Day Six

The Great Revelation of June 1675

"Then, discovering to me His divine Heart, He said: Behold this Heart, which has loved men so much, that It has spared nothing, even to exhausting and consuming Itself in order to testify to them Its love; and in return I receive from the greater number nothing but ingratitude by reason of their irreverence and sacrileges, and by the coldness and contempt which they show Me in this sacrament of love. But what I feel the most keenly is that it is hearts that are consecrated to Me that treat Me thus. Therefore, I ask of thee that the Friday after the Octave of Corpus Christi be set apart for a special feast to honor My Heart, by communicating on that day and making reparation to It by a solemn act, in order to make amends for the indignities which It has received during the time It has been exposed on the altars. I promise thee that My Heart shall expand itself to shed upon those who shall thus honor It, and cause It to be honored."

"In order to express the sacrificial offering of His Heart, He often showed me visibly the wound that He had received in His side; a crown of thorns surrounded His divine Heart. Once it was shown to me pierced through and through and wounded by blows; another time it was open like a bottomless abyss, an unfathomable depth torn open by the point of the lance. Usually the thorns of the crown enclosed it so tightly in a ring and pressed it with such force that it was thoroughly wounded.

"It was often revealed to me also as a glowing fire of love that purifies souls, like a glowing hearth and like a magnet that draws souls, like an abyss in which they must plunge if they wish to be renewed."

Testimonies of St. Margaret Mary Alacoque

Consideration

Let us listen to Our Lord's complaint: "My heart expected reproach and misery; I looked for sympathy, but there was none; and for comforters, and I found none."

Offertory for the Feast of the Sacred Heart of Jesus;
Psalm 68:21

Prayer of Reparation to the Most Sacred Heart of Jesus

O sweetest Jesus, whose overflowing charity towards men is most ungratefully repaid by such great forgetfulness, neglect, and contempt, see, prostrate before Thy altars, we strive by special honor to make amends for the wicked coldness of men and the contumely with which Thy most loving Heart is everywhere treated.

At the same time, mindful of the fact that we too have sometimes not been free from unworthiness, and moved therefore with most vehement sorrow, in the first place we implore Thy mercy on us, being prepared by voluntary expiation to make amends for the sins we have ourselves committed, and also for the sins of those who wander far from the way of salvation, whether because, being obstinate in their unbelief, they refuse to follow Thee as their shepherd and leader, or because, spurning the promises of their Baptism, they have cast off the most sweet yoke of Thy law.

We now endeavor to expiate all these lamentable crimes together, and it is also our purpose to make amends for each one of them severally: for the want of modesty in life and dress, for impurities, for so many snares set for the minds of the innocent, for the violation of feast days, for the horrid blasphemies against Thee and Thy saints, for the insults offered to Thy Vicar and to the priestly order, for the neglect of the sacrament of divine love or its profanation by horrible sacrileges, and lastly for the public sins of nations which resist the rights and the teaching authority of the Church which Thou hast instituted.

Would that we could wash away these crimes with our own blood! And now, to make amends for the outrage offered to the divine honor, we offer to Thee the same satisfaction which Thou didst once offer to Thy Father on the Cross and which Thou dost continually renew on our altars, we offer this conjoined with the expiations of the Virgin Mother and of all the saints, and of all pious Christians, promising from our heart that so far as in us lies, with the help of Thy grace, we will make amends for our own past sins, and for the sins of others, and for the neglect of Thy boundless love, by firm faith, by a pure way of life, and by a perfect observance of the Gospel law, especially that of charity; we will also strive with all our strength to prevent injuries being offered to Thee, and gather as many as we can to become Thy followers.

Pope Pius XI

Most Sacred Heart of Jesus, I place my trust in Thee!

Thought for the day
"Behold the Heart that loved mankind so much that It did not spare Itself but sacrificed and consumed Itself entirely, in order to prove to them Its love."

From the revelations to St. Margaret Mary

Day Seven

The Agony of the Heart of Jesus on the Mount of Olives

Meditation

"Jesus showed me His most loving and most amiable Heart. 'I will be thy strength,' He said to me, 'fear nothing, but be attentive to My voice and to what I shall require of thee.... Every night between Thursday and Friday I will make thee share in the mortal sadness which I was pleased to feel in the Garden of Olives.... And in order to bear Me company in the humble prayer that I then offered to My Father, in the midst of My anguish, thou shalt rise between eleven o'clock and midnight, and remain prostrate with Me for an hour, not only to appease divine anger by begging mercy for sinners, but also to mitigate in some way the bitterness which I felt at that time on finding Myself abandoned by My apostles, which obliged Me to reproach them for not being able to watch one hour with Me . . .'"

"No creature will ever be able to comprehend the greatness of the torment that I experienced then.... I suffered more interiorly there [in the Garden of Gethsemane] than in all the rest of My Passion, because I saw that I was abandoned by heaven and earth."

From the revelations to St. Margaret Mary

Consideration

This exhortation must be taken seriously. Jesus addresses it to us, although we are sinners and forget and offend Him again and again. He addresses it to all zealous souls who are willing to make atonement for the indifference and hostility of a God-forsaken world by their fidelity in faith, their love, and acts of reparation.

Act of Reparation to the Sacred Heart of Jesus

O divine Heart of Jesus, inexhaustible source of love and goodness, ah! how I regret that I have forgotten Thee so much and loved Thee so little! O Sacred Heart, Thou dost merit the reverence and love of all hearts which Thou hast cherished so much and laid under infinite obligations. And yet Thou dost receive from the greater number nothing but ingratitude and coldness, and especially from my own heart which merits Thy just indignation. But Thy Heart is all full of goodness and mercy, and of this I wish to avail myself to obtain reconciliation and pardon.

O divine Heart, I grieve intensely when I see myself guilty of such cowardice, and when I consider the ungrateful conduct of my wicked heart, which has so unjustly stolen the love that it owes to Thee and bestowed it on myself or on vain amusements.

O Heart most meek, if the sorrow and shame of a heart that recognizes its error can satisfy Thee, pardon this heart of mine for it is sorry for its infidelity and ashamed of the little care which it has taken to please Thee by its love.

O Sacred Heart of my Saviour, what could I expect from all this but Thy displeasure and condign punishment if I did not hope in Thy mercy. O Heart of my God, Heart most holy, Heart to which alone belongs to pardon sinners, do Thou in Thy mercy pardon this poor miserable heart of mine. All its powers unite in a supreme effort to make reparation to Thee for its wanderings from Thee and the disordered application of its love. Ah! how could I have been able hitherto to refuse Thee my heart, I who have so many obligations to make Thee its sole possessor, nevertheless I have done so.

But now I regret that I have wandered away from Thee, from the love of Thee who art the source of all goodness, in a word, from the Heart of my Jesus, who although needing me not, hast sought me out and lavished Thy favors on me.

O adorable Heart of Jesus, is it possible that my heart can have treated Thee thus, my heart which depends entirely on Thy love and Thy benefits and which, if Thou shouldst take them from it, would fall into the utmost extremes of misery or be reduced to nothingness? Ah! how I am beholden to Thy goodness, O indulgent Heart of my Saviour, for having borne with me so long in my ingratitude! Oh! how timely Thy mercies come to pardon my poor, inconstant heart!

O Heart of my Jesus, I now consecrate to Thee and give Thee all my love and the source of my love, which is my heart; I give Thee both irrevocably, although with great confusion for having so long refused Thee Thine own possessions.

O divine Heart, my very capability of bestowing my poor heart on Thee is a proof of Thy great love for me, but alas! I have availed myself badly of such a favorable opportunity to merit Thy love and grace. Oh! how great is my confusion at the thought of this!

O Heart of my Jesus, reform my faithless heart. Grant that henceforth it may bind itself to Thy love by its own, and that it may approach Thee as much in the future as it has wandered away from Thee in the past, and as Thou art the Creator of my heart, may Thou, I beseech Thee, one day give it the crown of immortality.

St. Margaret Mary Alacoque, Prayer no. 1

Most Sacred Heart of Jesus, I place my trust in Thee!

Thought for the Day

"No creature will ever be able to comprehend the greatness of the torment that I experienced then.... I suffered more interiorly there [in the Garden of Gethsemane] than in all the rest of My Passion, because I saw that I was abandoned by heaven and earth."

From the revelations to St. Margaret Mary

Day Eight

Trust in the Divine Heart of Jesus

Meditation

No grace is so great that we could not obtain it from the Heart of Jesus. The Savior promised this to His servant in these words: "Proclaim, and have it proclaimed to the whole world, that I set no limit on My gifts of grace for those who seek them in My Heart."

"The Most Sacred Heart of Jesus is the treasury of all graces, and trust is the key to it."

Testimonies of Saint Margaret Mary

Consideration

"You must think of how great God's goodness is, far beyond our imagining. Even when scruples arise, you must believe that you are loved by Him, despite all your misery. Keep these thoughts in your heart."

"Realize that all your faults are nothing in comparison to what you do if you lack trust in God. Hope to the end, I command you. If you obey me in this point, I guarantee that you will convert.... The more miserable we are, the more God is honored by the trust that we have in Him."

From the spiritual direction in the letters of St. Claude de La Colombière, the confessor of St. Margaret Mary Alacoque

Prayer of Trust

O Lord, "No one has hoped in Thee and has been confounded." (Psalm 24). I am assured, therefore, of my eternal happiness, for I firmly hope for it, and all my hope is in Thee. "In Thee, O Lord, I have hoped; let me never be confounded."

I know, alas! I know but too well that I am frail and changeable; I know the power of temptation against the strongest virtue. I have seen stars fall from heaven, and pillars of firmament totter; but these things alarm me not. While I hope in Thee I am sheltered from all misfortune, and I am sure that my trust shall endure, for I rely upon Thee to sustain this unfailing hope.

Finally, I know that my confidence cannot exceed Thy bounty, and that I shall never receive less than I have hoped for from Thee. Therefore I hope that Thou wilt sustain me against my evil inclinations; that Thou wilt protect me against the most furious assaults of the evil one, and that Thou wilt cause my weakness to triumph over my most powerful enemies. I hope that Thou wilt never cease to love me, and that I shall love Thee unceasingly. And so as to offer Thee as much hope as I can, I hope in Thee through Thyself, O my Creator and Lord, for time and eternity. Amen.

Prayer of St. Claude de la Colombière

Litany of the Passion

Humbly prostrate at the foot of Thy holy Cross, I will often say to Thee, in order to excite Thy compassion and obtain mercy and pardon:

Jesus, unknown and despised, have mercy on me.

Jesus, calumniated and persecuted, have mercy on me.

Jesus, abandoned by men, and tempted, have mercy on me.

Jesus, betrayed and sold for a paltry sum, have mercy on me.

Jesus, blamed, accused, and unjustly condemned, have mercy on me.

Jesus, clothed with a garment of opprobrium and shame, have mercy on me.

Jesus, buffeted and mocked, have mercy on me.

Jesus, dragged with a rope round Thy neck, have mercy on me.

Jesus, scourged unto blood, have mercy on me.

Jesus, reputed to be a fool and to be possessed by a devil, have mercy on me.

Jesus, to whom Barabbas was preferred, have mercy on me.

Jesus, shamefully stripped of Thy garments, have mercy on me.

Jesus, crowned with thorns and saluted in derision, have mercy on me.

Jesus, laden with the Cross, and disowned by Thy people, have mercy on me.

Jesus, overwhelmed with insults, sorrow, and humiliations, have mercy on me.

Jesus, sorrowful unto death, have mercy on me.

Jesus, insulted, spat upon, beaten, outraged, and scoffed at, have mercy on me.

Jesus, hanged on the infamous tree in company with robbers, have mercy on me.

Jesus, set at nought, and deprived of honor before men, have mercy on me.

Jesus, overwhelmed with all kinds of sorrow, have mercy on me.

O Good Jesus, who hast suffered an infinity of insults and humiliations for love of me, imprint deeply on my heart a great love and appreciation for them, and the desire to endure them willingly for Thee. Amen.

St. Margaret Mary Alacoque, Prayer no. 6

Most Sacred Heart of Jesus, I place my trust in You!

Thought for the day

"Sinners shall find in My Heart the source and infinite ocean of mercy."

From the promises to St. Margaret Mary

Day Nine

Consecration to the Sacred Heart of Jesus

Meditation

In many letters, Saint Margaret Mary Alacoque earnestly recommends consecration to the Most Sacred Heart of Jesus: "He has strengthened me in the conviction that He takes great pleasure in being loved, known, and honored by His creatures. This pleasure is so great that . . . He promised me that all those who are devoted and consecrated to Him will never be lost."

Letter no. 36 to Mother Greyfié in Semur, 1685

Consideration

"What does it mean for a family to be consecrated to the Heart of Jesus? Consecration means complete dedication of oneself to the Person of Jesus. Someone who consecrates himself, however, must also fulfill the duties that result from such an offering. If the Most Sacred Heart of Jesus really reigns in a family, then the persons and things in this sanctified home must be supported by an atmosphere of faith and piety. In a family that has consecrated itself to the Heart of Jesus, the parents and children feel familiar with God under God's watchful eyes. And therefore they are His messengers and obedient to the precepts of the Church. Before the picture of their heavenly King they fearlessly take upon themselves everything that their daily duties require of them, all the toils of their everyday routine, all their sacrifices in difficulties, and all the trials that God allows."

Pope Pius XII

Little Act of Consecration to the Sacred Heart of Jesus

I, —N—, give and consecrate to the Sacred Heart of our Lord Jesus Christ, my person and my life, my actions, penances, and sufferings, not wishing to make use of any part of my being for the future except in honoring, loving and glorifying that Sacred Heart. It is my irrevocable will to be entirely His and to do everything for His love, and I renounce with my whole heart whatever might displease Him.

I take Thee, then, O most Sacred Heart, as the sole object of my love, as the protector of my life, as the pledge of my salvation, as the remedy of my frailty and inconstancy, as the repairer of all the defects of my life, and as my secure refuge at the hour of my death.

Be then, O Heart of Goodness, my justification before God the Father, and remove far from me the thunderbolts of His just wrath.

O Heart of love, I place my whole confidence in Thee. While I fear all things from my malice and frailty, I hope all things from Thy goodness. Consume then in me whatever can displease or be opposed to Thee, and may Thy pure love be so deeply impressed on my heart that it may be impossible that I should ever be separated from Thee, or forget Thee.

I implore Thee, by Thy goodness, that my name may be written in Thee, for in Thee I wish to place all my happiness and all my glory, living and dying in very bondage to Thee. Amen.

St. Margaret Mary Alacoque, Prayer no. 25.

Consecration of the World to the Most Sacred Heart of Jesus

Most sweet Jesus, Redeemer of the human race, look down upon us humbly prostrate before Thine altar. We are Thine, and Thine we wish to be; but, to be more surely united with Thee, behold each one of us freely dedicates himself today to Thy most Sacred Heart.

Many indeed have never known Thee; many too, despising Thy precepts, have rejected Thee. Have mercy on them all, most merciful Jesus, and draw them to Thy Sacred Heart. Be Thou King, O Lord, not only of the faithful who have never forsaken Thee, but also of the prodigal sons who have abandoned Thee; grant that they may quickly return to Thy Father's house lest they perish of wretchedness and hunger.

Be Thou King of those whom heresy holds in error, or discord keeps aloof, and call them back to the harbor of truth and unity of faith, so that there may be one fold under the same one Shepherd.

Be Thou King of all those who even now sit in the shadow of idolatry or Islam, and refuse not to draw them into the light of Thy kingdom. Look finally with eyes of pity eyes of pity upon the children of that race, which was for so long a time Thy chosen people: and let Thy Blood, which was once invoked upon them in vengeance, now descend upon them in a cleansing flood of redemption and eternal life.

Grant, O Lord, to Thy Church assurance of freedom and immunity from harm; unto to all nations grant an ordered tranquillity, and bring it to pass that from pole to pole the earth may resound with one cry: "Praise be to the divine Heart that wrought our salvation; to it be honor and glory and for ever and ever. Amen.

Pope Leo XIII

Most Sacred Heart of Jesus, I place my trust in You!

Thought for the day

"When we are completely consecrated and pledged to this adorable Heart, to love and honor It as much as we can, abandoning ourselves entirely to It, our Lord takes care of us and sees to it that, in spite of all the storms, we come safely into the harbor of salvation.... If only people knew how useful and glorious it is to honor this most lovable Heart, and what the reward is for those who have consecrated themselves to It and seek to honor It!"

From the promises to St. Margaret Mary

At the Conclusion of the Novena

Lord Jesus Christ, I pay You homage as the king of the world. Everything that is created was created for You. Do with me whatever You will! I renew my baptismal vows, I renounce the devil, and all his works and pomps, and promise to live as a good Christian. In particular I pledge to collaborate, to the best of my ability, so that the rights of God and of Your Church might be victorious. Divine Heart of Jesus, to You I consecrate the little that I do, so that all hearts might acknowledge Your holy kingship and thus Your reign of peace might be firmly established throughout the world. Amen.

Indulgenced prayer of Pope Pius XI

Note for Families Consecrated to the Sacred Heart
At this point, we wish to remind you to inform the member of the Sacred Heart Family who is scheduled next, so that the perpetual novena might be continued without interruption.

Image of the Pierced Side of Christ / The Master of
Hohenfurth

Appendix I

Various Prayers

Litany of the Most Sacred Heart of Jesus

Lord, have mercy on us. *Christ, have mercy on us.*

Lord, have mercy on us. Christ, hear us. *Christ, graciously hear us.*

God, the Father of Heaven, *Have mercy on us.*

God the Son, Redeemer of the world, *Have mercy on us.*

God the Holy Ghost, *Have mercy on us.*

Holy Trinity, One God, *Have mercy on us.*

Heart of Jesus, Son of the Eternal Father, *Have mercy on us.*

Heart of Jesus, formed by the Holy Ghost in the womb of the Virgin Mother, *Have mercy on us.*

Heart of Jesus, substantially united to the Word of God, *etc.*

Heart of Jesus, of infinite majesty,

Heart of Jesus, holy temple of God,

Heart of Jesus, tabernacle of the Most High,

Heart of Jesus, house of God and gate of Heaven,

Heart of Jesus, burning furnace of charity,

Heart of Jesus, vessel of justice and love,

Heart of Jesus, full of goodness and love,

Heart of Jesus, abyss of all virtues,

Heart of Jesus, most worthy of all praise,

Heart of Jesus, king and center of all hearts,

Heart of Jesus, in Whom are all the treasures of wisdom and knowledge,

Heart of Jesus, in Whom dwelleth all the fullness of the divinity,

Heart of Jesus, in Whom the Father was well pleased,

Heart of Jesus, of Whose fullness we have all received,

Heart of Jesus, desire of the everlasting hills,

Heart of Jesus, patient and abounding in mercy,

Heart of Jesus, rich unto all who call upon Thee,

Heart of Jesus, fountain of life and holiness,

Heart of Jesus, propitiation for our sins,

Heart of Jesus, filled with reproaches,

Heart of Jesus, bruised for our iniquities,

Heart of Jesus, obedient even unto death,

Heart of Jesus, pierced with a lance,

Heart of Jesus, source of all consolation,

Heart of Jesus, our life and resurrection,

Heart of Jesus, our peace and reconciliation,

Heart of Jesus, victim for our sins,

Heart of Jesus, salvation of those who hope in Thee,

Heart of Jesus, hope of those who die in Thee,

Heart of Jesus, delight of all the saints,

Lamb of God, Who takest away the sins of the world,
Spare us, O Lord.

Lamb of God, Who takest away the sins of the world,
Graciously hear us, O Lord.

Lamb of God, Who takest away the sins of the world,
Have mercy on us.

V. Jesus, meek and humble of heart,

R. *Make our hearts like unto Thine.*

Let us pray.

Almighty and eternal God, consider the Heart of Thy well-beloved Son and the praises and satisfaction He offers Thee in the name of sinners; appeased by worthy homage, pardon those who implore Thy mercy, in the name of the same Jesus Christ Thy Son, Who lives and reigns with Thee, world without end. R. *Amen.*

Prayer of the Day from the Mass of the Sacred Heart of Jesus

O God, You mercifully deign to bestow on us in the Heart of Your Son, wounded by our sins, an infinite treasure of love; grant, we beseech You, that rendering It the devout homage of our affection, we may also make a worthy reparation for our sins. Through Christ our Lord. Amen.

Most Sacred Heart of Jesus, source of all good

Most Sacred Heart of Jesus, source of all good, I adore You, I believe in You, I hope in You and love You, and I am sorry for all my sins. I give to You this poor heart of mine. Make it humble, patient, pure and obedient to Your every wish.

O good Jesus, grant that I may live in You and You in me. Protect me in dangers, console me in sorrow and distress, and grant me health in body and soul, Your blessing on all my works and the grace of a happy death. Amen.

Indulgenced prayer of Pope Benedict XV, Brief dated December 4, 1915

Morning Offering

Everything for You, O Sacred Heart of Jesus! Mindful of Your love for me, I offer You today my prayers and works, joys and sufferings, all in union with the sacrifice that You offered on the cross to Your heavenly Father and renew each day on our altars, in reparation for my sins and for the extension of Your kingdom on earth. Amen.

Hymn: A Message From the Sacred Heart

A message from the Sacred Heart;
What may its message be?
"My Child, My Child, give Me thy heart
My Heart has bled for thee."
This is the message Jesus sends
To my poor heart today,
And eager from His Throne He bends
To hear what I shall say.

A message to the Sacred Heart;
Oh, bear it back with speed;
"Come, Jesus, reign within my heart;
Thy Heart is all I need."
Thus, Lord, I'll pray until I share
That home whose joy Thou art;
No message, dearest Jesus, there,
For heart will speak to heart.

Ejaculations
(A partial indulgence is gained every time these ejaculations are prayed.)

Most Sacred Heart of Jesus, I place my trust in You!

Most Sacred Heart of Jesus, I believe that You love me!

O loving Heart of my Jesus, grant that I may love You more and more!

Heart of Jesus, burning with love for us, kindle our hearts with love for You!

Jesus, meek and humble of heart, make our hearts like unto Thine!

All for You, O Most Sacred Heart of Jesus!

Most Sacred Heart of Jesus, grant that all may know, love, and imitate You!

Loving Heart of Jesus, be my love!

May the Most Sacred Heart of Jesus be loved everywhere!

Most Sacred Heart of Jesus, I consecrate myself to You through Mary!

Most Sacred Heart of Jesus, You were strengthened in Your agony by an angel. Strengthen us too in the hour of our death!

Most Sacred Heart of Jesus, have mercy on us!

Hymn: All You Who Seek a Comfort Sure
>All you who seek a comfort sure
>In trouble and distress,
>Whatever sorrow burdens you,
>Whatever griefs oppress.

Jesus, who gave Himself for you
Upon the Cross to die,
Opens to you His Sacred Heart;
O, to that Heart draw nigh.

You hear how kindly He invites;
You hear His words so blest:
"All you who labour, come to Me,
And I will give you rest."

O Heart adored by saints on high,
And hope of sinners here,
We place our humble trust in You
And lift to You our prayer.

Jesus, who gave Himself for you
Upon the Cross to die,
Let there His Heart for love be pierced:
O, to that Heart draw nigh!

Evening Offering

Saint Gertrude was once worried about the failings and omissions of which she had been guilty over the course of the day, and she turned to the Savior. Looking down from His Cross, the Lord answered her: "What you neglected to do, I have supplied for you. At every hour of this day, I pondered in My Heart what you should have considered and done, and in this way, It became so full of graces for you that it is as if overflowing, and with great impatience I awaited the moment in which you would address this prayer to Me. For otherwise nothing of what I gathered for you could have done you any good. Through this prayer, however, you can take it as your own in the sight of God, My Father."

With These Remorseful and Trusting Sentiments, we too may Certainly Pray:

Eternal Father, I offer You the Sacred Heart of Jesus, Your dearly-beloved Son, with all the pains and sorrows that He suffered for our salvation, to expiate all the sins I have committed this day and during all my life. *Glory be to the Father....*

Eternal Father, I offer You the Sacred Heart of Jesus, Your dearly-beloved Son, with all the love with which He performed His works on earth, to purify the good I have done poorly this day and during all my life. *Glory be to the Father....*

Eternal Father, I offer You the Sacred Heart of Jesus, Your dearly-beloved Son, with all His merits, to supply for the good I ought to have done and that I have neglected this day and during all my life. *Glory be to the Father....*

The Sacred Heart of Jesus, an Abyss of Wisdom and Love

The Sacred Heart of Jesus is an abyss of love, in which we must lose all other love, especially self-love and its evil fruits, such as human respect and the desire to follow our own inclinations.

If you are in an abyss of privation and desolation, enter into this divine Heart. There is all consolation, and we must plunge ourselves into this abyss, without, however, desiring to taste of its sweetness, unless it pleases Him.

If you are in an abyss of resistance and opposition to the divine will, plunge yourself into the abyss of submission and conformity to the divine pleasure which you will find in the Sacred Heart, and there, losing your resistance, you will clothe yourself with conformity to His will in all that may happen to you.

If you are in an abyss of dryness and weakness, go and bury yourself in the loving Heart of Jesus, which is an abyss of power within you, without desiring to taste of its sweetness, unless it pleases Him.

If you are in an abyss of poverty and stripped of all things, bury yourself in the Heart of Jesus; He will enrich you and fill you with joy, if you allow it.

If you find yourself in an abyss of weakness so that you fall at every step, go and bury yourself in the strength of His Sacred Heart, He will strengthen you and often cheer you again.

If you are in an abyss of misery, bury it in the mercies of this adorable Heart, and as you lose your wretchedness in them, regard yourself as a creature of His mercies.

If you fall into an abyss of pride and vain self-esteem, bury them immediately in the abyss of the humility of the Sacred Heart, in which you must lose all overweening presumption, and clothe yourself with His holy self-denial through the confession of your wretchedness.

If you are in an abyss of ignorance, go and plunge yourself into the loving Heart of Jesus, which is an abyss of knowledge. He will teach you how to love and please Him.

If you find yourself in an abyss of infidelity and inconstancy, bury yourself in the abyss of the constancy and stability of the Sacred Heart of Jesus, our loyal, true friend, who will teach us to be faithful to Him continually, as He always was to us in His love.

If you find yourself in an abyss of poverty, bury yourself in fullness of all the treasures of the adorable Heart of Jesus, and lose yourself therein as though in an inexhaustible source, and through true mortification find there a wellspring of life, so that you now look only with the eyes of Jesus, and hear only with His ears, and speak only with His tongue and love only through His lovable Heart.

If you find yourself in an abyss of ingratitude for the great gifts you have received from God, go and hide yourself in the divine Heart, which is a source of gratitude, with which He will fill you. Ask Him to supply for you and to give you what you owe to Him.

If you find yourself in an abyss of agitation, impatience, or anger, go and bury yourself in the sweetness of the loving Heart of Jesus, so that He may make you meek and humble of heart like Himself.

If you are in an abyss of distractions, bury them in the abyss of the tranquility of the Sacred Heart, and He will infallibly gain the victory for you, if you generously fight the distractions.

If you are in an abyss of spiritual darkness, bury yourself in the light of His divine Heart; there you will lose your darkness and He will clothe you with His light, so that you can give yourself up to His guidance like a blind man who now wants to see everything only in this divine light.

If you feel that you are plunged into an abyss of sadness, go and lose yourself in the divine joy of the Sacred Heart; there you will find a treasure of joy which will dispel all the sadness and gloom of your mind.

If you are in trouble and anxiety, go and plunge yourself into the peace of His adorable Heart, which no one can take from you.

If you are in an abyss of fear, bury yourself in the abyss of the trust of the Sacred Heart, there let your fear give way to love.

If you feel that you are in an abyss of ill-humor and discontent, bury yourself in the Sacred Heart, so as to lose yourself therein and rejoice in Him alone.

If you are in an abyss of bitterness and sorrows, bury yourself in the Sacred Heart of Jesus, so as to unite them with His; there you will find a treasure of joy that will make you submissive to His will, so that you may suffer everything silently, without complaining.

Often plunge yourself into the charity of this lovable Heart, so that you may never do anything to your neighbor that could wound this virtue, and never do to others what you would not want them to do to you.

You can plunge into the Heart of Jesus also as though into an abyss of purity and perfection, so as to purify your intentions and perfect your desires and resolutions, renounce your life of sinfulness and imperfection, and find the life of grace, charity, and perfection for which It destines you.

Oh, lose yourself in this sacred abyss and never leave it again; then it will soften your hardened heart and make it receptive to His graces and love.

Invocations to the Sacred Heart of Jesus After Holy Communion

O Most Sacred Heart of Jesus,

With Your all-encompassing love—I unite myself.

With Your steadfast trust—I unite myself.

With Your burning zeal—I unite myself.

With Your profound adoration—I unite myself.

With Your thanksgiving—I unite myself.

With Your satisfaction—I unite myself.

With Your ardent prayers—I unite myself.

With Your humility—I unite myself.

With Your obedience—I unite myself.

With Your meekness and peace—I unite myself.

With Your deep recollection—I unite myself.

With Your eloquent silence—I unite myself.

With Your ineffable goodness—I unite myself.

With Your loving care for the conversion of sinners—I unite myself.

With Your will, Your desires, and Your intentions—I unite myself.

With Your interior union with Your Heavenly Father—I unite myself.

Love of the Heart of Jesus—inflame my heart.

Compassion of the Heart of Jesus—pour Yourself into my heart.

Strength of the Heart of Jesus—strengthen my heart.

Mercy of the Heart of Jesus—forgive my heart.

Patience of the Heart of Jesus—bear with my heart.

Dominion of the Heart of Jesus—take possession of my heart.

Wisdom of the Heart of Jesus—instruct my heart.

Will of the Heart of Jesus—take control over my heart.

Zeal of the Heart of Jesus—consume my heart.
Immaculate Virgin Mary—pray for us to the Sacred
Heart of Jesus.

Holy Hour on Thursday Evening

This devotion was requested by our Savior:
to watch with Him for one hour and console
Him during His agony in the Garden of Olives
(see the meditation on day seven of the novena).
It is desirable to spend this hour of watching and
praying in church together as a public devotion.
However, since it is usually not possible to hold this
Holy Hour at the official time of 11:00 P.M.–12:00
A.M., it is permissible to schedule it at 6:00 P.M.
It is recommended that during this hour of prayer
the participants meditate on the agony of Jesus and
recite the Prayer of Atonement of Pope Pius XI (see
page 24–26).

Prayer to Jesus in the Garden of Gethsemane

O Jesus, through the abundance of Your love,
and in order to overcome our hardheartedness, You
pour out torrents of Your graces over those who
meditate on Your most sacred sorrow in the garden
of Gethsemane, and who spread devotion to You. I
pray You, move my soul and my heart to think often,
at least once a day, of Your most bitter agony in the
garden of Gethsemane, in order to communicate with
You and to be united with You as closely as possible.

O blessed Jesus, You, who carried the immense
burden of our sins that night, and atoned for them
fully, grant me the most perfect gift of complete
loving repentance for my numerous sins, for which
You sweated blood.

O blessed Jesus, for the sake of Your most bitter struggle in the Garden of Gethsemane, grant me final victory over all temptations, especially over those to which I am most subject.

O suffering Jesus, for the sake of Your inscrutable and indescribable agonies during that night of betrayal, and of Your bitterest anguish of mind, enlighten me, so that I may recognize and fulfill Your will, grant that I may ponder continually on Your heart-wrenching struggle and on how You emerged victorious, in order to fulfill not Your will, but the will of Your Father.

Blessed be You, O Jesus, for all Your sighs on that holy night, and for the tears which You shed for us.

Blessed be You, O Jesus, for Your sweat of blood and the terrible agony that You suffered lovingly in coldest abandonment and in inscrutable loneliness.

Blessed be You, O sweetest Jesus, filled with immeasurable bitterness, for the prayer which flowed in trembling agony from Your Heart, so truly human and divine.

Eternal Father, I offer You all the past, present, and future Masses in union with the blood of Christ shed in agony in the garden of sorrow at Gethsemane.

Most Holy Trinity, grant that the knowledge, and thereby the love, of the agony of Jesus on the Mount of Olives will spread throughout the whole world.

Grant, O Jesus, that all who look lovingly at You on the Cross, will also remember Your immense suffering on the Mount of Olives, that they will follow Your example, learn to pray devoutly and fight victoriously, so that, one day, they may be able to glorify You eternally in Heaven. Amen.

Attributed to Saint Pio of Pietrelcina; approved by Bishop Macario, Fabiano, November 23, 1963

Prayers of Atonement Taught by the Angel of Fatima

My God, I believe in You, I adore You, I hope in You, and I love You. I ask pardon for all those who do not believe in You, do not adore You, do not hope in You, and do not love You.

Most Holy Trinity, Father, Son, and Holy Ghost, I adore You profoundly, and I offer You the Most Precious Body, Blood, Soul, and Divinity of our Lord Jesus Christ, truly present in all the tabernacles of the world, in reparation for the outrages, sacrileges, and indifferences by which He Himself is offended. By the infinite merits of His Most Sacred Heart, and through the Immaculate Heart of Mary, I beg of Thee the conversion of poor sinners.

Act of Consecration of the Family: Enthronement of the Sacred Heart of Jesus

The following act of consecration was approved by Pope Saint Pius X on May 18, 1908. During the enthronement ceremony, the act of consecration is recited by the head of the family together with those present:

O Sacred Heart of Jesus, who made known to Saint Margaret Mary Your ardent desire to reign over Christian families, behold us assembled here today to proclaim Your absolute dominion over our home.

Henceforth we resolve to lead a life like Yours so that among us may flourish the virtues for which You promised peace on earth, and for this end we will banish from our midst the spirit of the world which You abhor so much.

May You reign over our understanding by the simplicity of our faith. May You reign over our hearts by an ardent love for You; and may the flame of this love be ever kept burning in our hearts by the frequent reception of the Holy Eucharist.

Deign, O divine Heart, to preside over our meetings, to bless our undertakings, both spiritual and temporal, to banish all worry and care, to sanctify our joys, and soothe our sorrows. If any of us should ever have the misfortune to grieve Your Sacred Heart, remind him of Your goodness and mercy toward the repentant sinner.

Lastly, when the hour of separation will sound and death will plunge our home into mourning, then shall we all and every one of us be resigned to Your eternal decrees, and seek consolation in the thought that we shall all one day be reunited in heaven, where we shall sing the praises and blessings of Your Sacred Heart for all eternity.

May the Immaculate Heart of Mary and the glorious patriarch Saint Joseph offer You this our consecration and remind us of the same all the days of our life.

Glory to the divine Heart of Jesus, our King! Amen.

Prayer for the Renewal of the Sacred Heart Enthronement

Most Sweet Jesus, humbly kneeling at Your feet, we renew the consecration of our family to Your divine Heart. Be our king forever! In You we have full and complete confidence. May Your spirit penetrate our thoughts, our desires, our words, and our works.

Bless our undertakings, share in our joys, in our trials and our labors. Grant that we may know You better, love You more, and serve You without faltering. May the same cry resound from one end of the earth to the other: May the triumphant Heart of Jesus be loved, blessed, and glorified everywhere and forever! Amen.

Cardinal Mercier

"Father, if thou wilt, remove this chalice from me;
but yet not my will, but thine be done." (Lk. 22:42)

The Sacred Heart of Jesus depicted with the
Twelve Promises

Appendix II

The Twelve Promises of Our Lord Jesus Christ to Saint Margaret Mary Alacoque for Those who Honor His Most Sacred Heart

The promises of the Sacred Heart are commonly known in a summarized or abridged form, which contains the following twelve points:

1. I will bless the homes where an image of My Heart shall be exposed and honored.
2. I will establish peace in their families.
3. I will console them in all their troubles.
4. They shall find in My Heart an assured refuge during life and especially at the hour of their death.
5. I will pour abundant blessings on all their undertakings.
6. Sinners shall find in My Heart the source of an infinite ocean of mercy.
7. Tepid souls shall become fervent.

8. Fervent souls shall speedily rise to great perfection.

9. I will give them all the graces necessary for their state in life.

10. I will give to priests the power of touching the most hardened hearts.

11. Those who propagate this devotion shall have their names written in My Heart, never to be effaced.

12. The all-powerful love of My Heart will grant the grace of final repentance to all those who shall receive Communion on the First Friday of nine consecutive months (in the state of sanctifying grace); they shall not die under my displeasure, nor without receiving their sacraments; My heart shall be their assured refuge at that last hour.

The Detailed Version of the Promises According to the Saint's Authentic Writings

In the following pages we reprint some of the exact quotations of this legacy of love, taken from the writings of St. Margaret Mary Alacoque. They are cited from *Vie et oeuvres de sainte Marguerite-Marie Alacoque,* 3 vols. (Paris, 1920), with references to the volume and page number.

The promises for those who honor the divine Heart are comprehensive. For every state in life and for every state of soul the Savior promises the necessary graces for conversion, for the divinely willed fulfillment of our task in life, for progress on the way to holiness and for perfection in love.

General Promise for all Believers

"I doubt whether there is any exercise of piety in the spiritual life as well adapted to raise a soul to the highest perfection in a short time and to make it taste the true sweetness one finds in the service of Jesus Christ. Yes, I am certain that if people knew how pleasing this devotion is to Jesus Christ, there would not be a Christian with so little love for this lovable Savior as not to practice it at once."

Letter no. 141 to Fr. Croiset, II:627

For Those who Work for the Salvation of Souls

"My divine Redeemer gave me to understand that all who work for the salvation of souls will have the gift of touching even the most hardened hearts. They will work with marvelous success, if only they themselves practice a loving devotion to His Sacred Heart and strive to spread and establish the same devotion everywhere. But for this purpose they must derive all their light from this Most Sacred Heart as their source." (II:439, 407, 628)

"It is enough to make the divine Heart known and then to leave to Him the trouble of permeating the hearts that He has reserved for Himself with the anointing of His grace; blessed are they who are in that number!" (II:490)

"There is nothing sweeter and milder, and at the same time nothing stronger and more efficacious than the gentle unction of the burning charity of this lovable Heart, to convert the most hardened souls and to penetrate the most unfeeling hearts with the word of Its heralds and true friends, which will make it a fiery sword that will melt the iciest heart in Its love." (II:557)

For Those who Want to Improve

"I am confident that this divine Heart is an overflowing, inexhaustible source of mercy and grace with which to appease God's righteous anger over so many sins. With respect to the love that He has for this Most Sacred Heart, God will forgive sinners. This divine Heart is a fortress and a sure refuge for all who would take shelter therein, to avoid the strokes of divine justice. (II:363, 429)

"The most effective means that we have to lift ourselves up again from our fall into sin is the Most Sacred Heart of our Lord Jesus Christ." (II:159)

"The Sacred Heart is almighty to obtain mercy." (II:300)

"The Sacred Heart wants to destroy Satan's kingdom in souls, so as to establish the kingdom of His love there." (II:437, 363, 489)

For Religious Communities

"He promised me that He will pour out the gentle anointing of His fiery love upon all communities in which His divine image is honored and which place themselves under His special protection. He will divert from them the punishments of divine justice and renew their zeal, if they have lost it." (II:296, 300, 532)

"He wants to keep all hearts united, so as to be one with those who are His." (II:533)

"No other means is necessary in order to restore less edifying religious communities to their initial zeal and the most faithful observance of the rule, and to lead those who were living in strict observance of the rule to the utmost perfection." (II:627)

"How many blessings and graces He has resolved to pour out on the communities that offer Him more honor and glory!" (II:431)

For Souls of Good will

"People living in the world will find all the help necessary for their state in life by means of this lovable devotion." (II:627)

"He will grant peace to their families, reunite divided families, and assist and protect those that are in any sort of need." (II:296, 300)

"He will support them in their labors. In time of need, He will protect and console them. Over all their endeavors, He will pour out His blessings." (II:628)

"In this Heart, they will find their refuge in life, but especially at the hour of their death." (II:628)

"How easy death is, after one has practiced a constant devotion to the Heart that will judge us!" (II:628)

"Those who practice the devotion to this Most Sacred Heart will not be lost, for a child cannot perish in the arms of an almighty Father." (II:411, 328, 528, 386)

For Those who Consecrate Themselves to the Sacred Heart

"If people only knew how beneficial and glorious it is to honor this lovable heart, and what the reward is for those who have consecrated themselves to It and seek to honor It!" (II:279)

"If we have consecrated ourselves entirely to this lovable Heart, He will take care of us and bring us to the harbor of salvation, despite all storms." (II:291)

"Anyone who surrenders entirely to God by consecrating himself to the Most Sacred Heart of Jesus, will be assured of salvation." (II:298)

"I cannot believe that persons who are consecrated to the Sacred Heart of Jesus could perish, nor that they will fall into Satan's power through mortal sin, if only they are guided in all things by His holy precepts." (II:328)

"It seems to me that there is no more certain means of salvation than to be entirely consecrated to the divine Heart. Not one of those who are especially devoted and consecrated to It will be lost." (cf. II:344, 345-346)

For Apostles of the Sacred Heart of Jesus

"He let me see many names that are inscribed on His Sacred Heart because of their desire to promote devotion to It; therefore He will never allow them to be blotted out from It." (II: 303, 408)

"He disclosed to me treasures of love and of grace for those who consecrate and sacrifice themselves to give and procure for Him all the honor, love, and glory in their power." (II:396)

For Homes in which His Image is Honored

"Since Jesus is the source of all blessings, He will pour them out abundantly upon all places where the image of His lovable Heart is displayed to be loved and honored." (II:296, 300, 532)

"He promised me that He will abundantly pour out all the treasures of the graces with which He is filled into the hearts of those who honor the image of His Most Sacred Heart; and wherever this image is displayed and honored in a special way, it will call down all sorts of blessings." (I:244)

For the Special Celebration of the Feast of the Sacred Heart of Jesus

"I ask of you that a special feast to honor My Heart be instituted on the first Friday after the Octave of Corpus Christi.... I promise you that My Heart will shower with the stream of Its divine love those who show It this honor and teach others to do so." (II:103)

"This feast is a day of salvation and of eternal blessings for all who honor It with a humble and sincere heart. (II:444, 439)

To Make the Nine First Fridays in Honor of the Sacred Heart

"I promise you, in the superabundance of My mercy, that in My all-powerful love I will grant to everyone who communicates on nine consecutive first Fridays of the month the grace of final repentance. They will not die in My disfavor, nor without receiving the sacraments. My divine Heart shall be their sure refuge in their final hour."

Letter no. 86 to Mother de Saumaise at Dijon, May 1688, II:397 and 1:261

Note: The sequence of the nine First Fridays must be uninterrupted. In order to share in the promised effects, the holy communions must be received with the intention of honoring the Sacred Heart of Jesus and making reparation to Him for all the insults and ingratitude that He endures. It is enough, however, to formulate this intention once explicitly at the beginning of the practice; it is unnecessary to renew the intention specially each time. These holy communions must be received worthily, that is, in the state of grace. Therefore another part of this devotional atonement is the worthy reception of sacramental confession as a preparation for the communion of reparation. The confession does not necessarily have to be made on the first Friday of the month; it can also occur in the week before or afterward.

Promise That the Kingdom of the Sacred Heart of Jesus will Come

"Fear nothing, I shall reign in spite of My enemies, and of all who oppose Me." (II:105 / *Autobiography*)

"This lovable Heart will reign, in spite of Satan. This saying fills me with joy and it's all my consolation."

"Finally this divine Heart will triumph despite those who try to oppose It. Satan and his minions will fall back in confusion. How happy then will they be whom He has employed to build up His kingdom. The adorable Heart of Jesus wishes to establish His reign of love in all hearts, and to destroy Satan's kingdom." (II: 436, 489)

> *"Heaven and earth shall pass,*
> *but My words shall not pass."*
> *(Mt. 24:35)*

Appendix III

The Heart of Jesus Family

The prayer group of the Heart of Jesus Family [*Famille du Coeur de Jesus*] is an extremely valuable apostolate for the sanctification of families through the divine Heart of Jesus. It consists of fourteen prayer partners or families who join together as a family group and take turns praying year-round as a spiritual community, a perpetual novena to the Most Sacred Heart of Jesus.

In this way, perpetual honor and continual reparation is offered for the insults against the Sacred Heart of Jesus and the Immaculate Heart of Mary.

The Origin of This Prayer Association

The Association of the Heart of Jesus Family was founded in 1971 in Canada by Father Pierre Gendron and has now spread to forty-two countries.

Since its founding, a great number of people have been making sure that uninterrupted prayer to the Lord our God rises up to heaven.

Today the movement is present on all five continents.

Structure of the Heart of Jesus Family

It is altogether essential that the Heart of Jesus Family be propagated in collaboration with priests and also through the lay apostolate. All are invited to profess their faith in Jesus Christ, the Son of God, in the presence of their brothers and sisters.

Prayer is the source of spiritual fruitfulness, and therefore people become actively involved and become "apostles" by forming prayer groups. The "apostle" who wants to start a new Heart of Jesus Family invites others to pray this novena with him and to help him recruit the necessary number of prayer partners or participating families for this apostolate.

A complete Heart of Jesus Family is composed of fourteen members, who are willing to make the novena in this book three times a year. The word "member" here means either an individual person or usually a family (father and/or mother and children), who pray together on the appointed days and can be regarded as a single member.

Anyone can join this prayer family. The only requirements are: the willingness to pray the novena faithfully, and the desire and intention to make reparation to the Heart of Jesus, and to promote this devotion.

The Threefold Purpose of the Heart of Jesus Family
1. Love

The Heart of Jesus Family was founded in order to revive and promote devotion to the Sacred Heart of Jesus, which had been very much neglected. In His Heart, the Savior reveals to us God's love for our time. The Heart of Jesus Family wishes to cooperate in making the Most Sacred Heart of Jesus better known again and loved by all people. Individuals who practice this devotion to the Heart of Jesus were certainly chosen and prompted by a special grace of this Heart of love. The more zealously and faithfully someone honors this Heart, the more he will be filled with His love!

2. Reparation

Another essential part of the devotion to the Heart of Jesus is atonement and reparation. The more we see lukewarmness, abuses, sins, public insults, and blasphemies against God and the Sacred Heart of Jesus in the Church and the world, the more resolved and eager we should be to atone for these insults and make reparation for them. This is done through the zealous recitation of the prayers, through faithful adherence to Christian ideals in daily life, and by voluntarily offering sacrifices for the love of God.

3. Apostolate

Another concern of the prayer family is to make this devotion known to their fellow men through prayer and a personal apostolate in the spirit of practical Christian love of neighbor, and thus to lead as many souls as possible to the Heart of Jesus, so that He can bestow on them His grace and mercy. Let us not forget the Lord's promise: "Those who propagate this devotion shall have their names written in My Heart, never to be effaced."

Saint Margaret Mary recorded the following vision about the salvation of souls through the Heart of Jesus: "[The divine Heart] was often revealed to me also as a glowing fire of love that purifies souls, like a glowing hearth, and like a magnet that draws souls, like an abyss in which they must plunge if they wish to be renewed.

"I saw souls that had grown cold and stiff (in sin), who approached this fire and suddenly, just when it seemed that they would be warmed, frantically fled and were lost in the darkness.

"Then I saw other souls come that were cold, ugly, and deformed at first (again because of sin), who brightened up upon coming into contact with the Heart of Jesus, were enkindled, and ended up being lost in Him like a spark in the fireplace of divine love."

One Necessary Condition: our Trust

Let us always pray with trust: this pleases God, for the Savior Himself exhorts us: "Ask, and it shall be given you; seek, and you shall find; knock, and it shall be opened to you" (Mt. 7:7). God wants to grant His benefits to those who urgently implore them.

Saint Gertrude attributed all the graces that she had received to her trust alone. Once as she asked the Lord for the salvation of a great number of sinners and did not dare to tell Him that these souls were in a state of mortal sin, the Savior gently rebuked her, because she had thereby tried to set limits on His Divine Mercy; and He said: "Trust alone can obtain all things easily." He granted her everything that she had asked Him for and added: "This is because it gives me such great joy when men hope for great things from Me. I will always answer their prayers beyond their expectations!"

Duties of the Heart of Jesus Families

The task of the members consists of praying the novena for nine days, three times a year, during the times scheduled on the calendar. The dates are indicated on the last page of this novena booklet. Upon arriving at the ninth day of his novena, the member notifies the member who is scheduled next, so that the novena is prayed uninterruptedly. In this way, it becomes a perpetual novena, which unites the members of this spiritual family. We are also invited and encouraged to pray for one another. Pointing out to one another the duty to pray, fosters the spiritual ties among the family members in their common love for Christ.

The Family of the Sacred Heart of Jesus accepts every new member joyfully, for all benefit spiritually from the prayer of the new family member.

The Leader (Apostle) of the Individual Group

The apostle determines the sequence and the dates for the individual members, which are scheduled on the calendar. When the number of members reaches fourteen, the prayer group is complete, and this makes the perpetual novena possible.

The apostle also has the responsibility of staying in contact with his members and making sure that they keep their assigned times of prayer. Above all he will ceaselessly urge all who participate to persevere in prayer. The fidelity and zeal of the apostle safeguard the constancy of this prayer that we wish to offer to the Heart of Jesus.

The Importance of Family Prayer

"A family that prays is a family that lives and stays together," said Pope Pius XII. If we want to rebuild society in the love of Christ, we must begin with prayer in the family, the basic cell of society.

Pope Pius XII confirms also that "devotion to the Most Sacred Heart of Jesus is the summary of the entire Catholic faith and therefore is absolutely necessary for the Christian family today." Everything comes from the Heart of Jesus: the Church, the forgiveness of sins, the Eucharist, the Holy Spirit, and the Virgin Mary, for on the cross Jesus said to John, and thus to all of us: "Behold your mother!"

The Heart of Jesus on the cross was pierced by a soldier's lance, and since then streams of love and mercy flow from It. "Out of his belly shall flow rivers of living water." (Jn. 7:37-39)

When Jesus appeared to Saint Margaret Mary Alacoque and showed her His Heart, He made great promises to all who would honor His Heart. Let us not, above all, forget this promise of the Lord: "Tepid souls shall become fervent. Fervent souls shall speedily rise to great perfection."

Enthronement of the Sacred Heart

At this point, we would like to recommend to all families the Enthronement of the Sacred Heart as well, whereby we dedicate ourselves entirely to the Heart of Jesus, place ourselves under His protection, and exalt Christ as king over our family. An introduction to it can be found in the leaflet entitled *Enthronement of the Sacred Heart in the Home* available at the address listed below. It calls for committed service to save the Christian family. The battle over the reign of Christ is being fought today in a particular way in the family. This is the decisive area. If the enemy were to achieve the de-Christianization of marital and family life, just as he has brought about the de-Christianization of public life, it would be easy for him to make Christianity disappear in many regions of the world.

Consequently, it is our task, if we really want to be soldiers for Christ's kingdom, deliberately to place the realm of the family under God's rule again, to recognize Christ's kingship in our marriages and in our families, and therefore to protect and foster religious practice in the family.

Invitation to Join the Heart of Jesus Family

Do you feel that the idea of the Heart of Jesus Family speaks to you? Would you like to join such a family or even found one yourself with your relatives or acquaintances?

Then send your inquiry to the following: Heart of Jesus Family Novena – P.O. Box 217 – Saint Mary's KS 66536. Please include your name, address and telephone number plus an email address if possible.

Adveniat regnum tuum –
Thy Kingdom come,
O Sacred Heart of Jesus!

Calandar for the Heart of Jesus Families Novena

1. Name_____Aug. 7–15 **8. Name**_____Oct. 9-17
Ph._____Dec. 7-15 Ph._____Feb. 8-16
Address_____Apr. 7-15 Address_____Jun. 9-17

---

2. Name_____Aug. 16-24 **9. Name**_____Oct. 18–26
Ph._____Dec. 16-24 Ph._____Feb. 17-25
Address_____Apr. 16-24 Address_____Jun. 18-26

---

3. Name_____Aug. 25-Sep. 2 **10. Name**_____Oct. 27–Nov. 4
Ph._____Dec. 25-Jan. 2 Ph._____Feb. 26 -Mar. 6
Address_____Apr. 25-May 3 Address_____Jun. 27-Jul. 5

---

4. Name_____Sep. 3-11 **11. Name**_____Nov. 5–13
Ph._____Jan. 3-11 Ph._____Mar. 7-15
Address_____May. 4-12 Address_____Jul. 6-14

---

5. Name_____Sep. 12–20 **12. Name**_____Nov. 14–22
Ph._____Jan. 12-20 Ph._____Mar. 16-24
Address_____May 13-21 Address_____Jul. 15-23

---

6. Name_____Sep. 21–29 **13. Name**_____Nov. 23–Dec. 1
Ph._____Jan. 21-29 Ph._____Mar. 25- Apr. 2
Address_____May 22-30 Address_____Jul. 24-Aug.1

---

7. Name_____Sep. 30–Oct. 8 **14. Name**_____Dec. 2–10
Ph._____Jan. 30-Feb. 7 Ph._____Apr. 3-11
Address_____May 31-Jun. 8 Address_____Aug. 2-10

Calandar for the Heart of Jesus Families Novena

1. Name_____	Aug. 7–15	8. Name_____	Oct. 9-17
Ph._____	Dec. 7-15	Ph._____	Feb. 8-16
Address_____	Apr. 7-15	Address_____	Jun. 9-17

2. Name_____	Aug. 16-24	9. Name_____	Oct. 18–26
Ph._____	Dec. 16-24	Ph._____	Feb. 17-25
Address_____	Apr. 16-24	Address_____	Jun. 18-26

3. Name_____	Aug. 25-Sep. 2	10. Name_____	Oct. 27–Nov. 4
Ph._____	Dec. 25-Jan. 2	Ph._____	Feb. 26 -Mar. 6
Address_____	Apr. 25-May 3	Address_____	Jun. 27-Jul. 5

4. Name_____	Sep. 3-11	11. Name_____	Nov. 5–13
Ph._____	Jan. 3-11	Ph._____	Mar. 7-15
Address_____	May. 4-12	Address_____	Jul. 6-14

5. Name_____	Sep. 12–20	12. Name_____	Nov. 14–22
Ph._____	Jan. 12-20	Ph._____	Mar. 16-24
Address_____	May 13-21	Address_____	Jul. 15-23

6. Name_____	Sep. 21–29	13. Name_____	Nov. 23–Dec. 1
Ph._____	Jan. 21-29	Ph._____	Mar. 25- Apr. 2
Address_____	May 22-30	Address_____	Jul. 24-Aug.1

7. Name_____	Sep. 30–Oct. 8	14. Name_____	Dec. 2–10
Ph._____	Jan. 30-Feb. 7	Ph._____	Apr. 3-11
Address_____	May 31-Jun. 8	Address_____	Aug. 2-10

Calandar for the Heart of Jesus Families Novena

1. Name_____Aug. 7–15
Ph._____Dec. 7-15
Address_____Apr. 7-15

2. Name_____Aug. 16-24
Ph._____Dec. 16-24
Address_____Apr. 16-24

3. Name_____Aug. 25-Sep. 2
Ph._____Dec. 25-Jan. 2
Address_____Apr. 25-May 3

4. Name_____Sep. 3-11
Ph._____Jan. 3-11
Address_____May. 4-12

5. Name_____Sep. 12-20
Ph._____Jan. 12-20
Address_____May 13-21

6. Name_____Sep. 21-29
Ph._____Jan. 21-29
Address_____May 22-30

7. Name_____Sep. 30–Oct. 8
Ph._____Jan. 30-Feb. 7
Address_____May 31-Jun. 8

8. Name_____Oct. 9-17
Ph._____Feb. 8-16
Address_____Jun. 9-17

9. Name_____Oct. 18–26
Ph._____Feb. 17-25
Address_____Jun. 18-26

10. Name_____Oct. 27–Nov. 4
Ph._____Feb. 26 -Mar. 6
Address_____Jun. 27-Jul. 5

11. Name_____Nov. 5–13
Ph._____Mar. 7-15
Address_____Jul. 6-14

12. Name_____Nov. 14–22
Ph._____Mar. 16-24
Address_____Jul. 15-23

13. Name_____Nov. 23–Dec. 1
Ph._____Mar. 25- Apr. 2
Address_____Jul. 24-Aug.1

14. Name_____Dec. 2–10
Ph._____Apr. 3-11
Address_____Aug. 2-10